The Wee Book of
EDINBURGH

Jan-Andrew Henderson

Black & White Publishing

First published 2004
by Black & White Publishing Ltd
99 Giles Street, Edinburgh EH6 6BZ

ISBN 1 84502 006 5

A CIP catalogue record for this book is available from The British Library.

Printed and bound in Spain by Bookprint, S.L., Barcelona.

INTRODUCTION

Edinburgh is a photographer's dream – a World Heritage Site and a city of great beauty and visible history. Walking down the historic Royal Mile or strolling through the Georgian splendour of the capital's New Town, it is easy to picture the Dickensian vagabonds, bewigged gentry and hairy Highlanders that once trod these very same streets.

What makes a photographic record of this city so fascinating is the fact that Edinburgh is a place of great contrasts – and it always has been. In the eighteenth and nineteenth centuries, it was known as the 'Athens of the North' and led the world in the arts and sciences. At the same time, it was notorious for having some of the worst poverty, overcrowding and crime in Europe. This collection of photographs captures the essence of a city that is ancient yet modern, conservative yet flamboyant, unique yet totally Scottish.

Jan-Andrew Henderson

The irregular skyline of the Old Town, with its domes and many spires towering high above the rest of the city, is instantly recognisable as Edinburgh. In fact, this part of the city is built on a glaciated ridge that slopes up to Edinburgh Castle and then plummets down a sheer cliff face into the city again.

For hundreds of years, the Old Town was Edinburgh – the city did not really begin to expand until the eighteenth century. The result was a huge population crammed into a very small area – at one time there were 80,000 people living in an area roughly one mile long and a quarter of a mile wide.

The buildings that sprang up to cope with this influx and the social conditions it spawned were interesting to say the least – as many of the following photographs demonstrate.

*Taken in the late nineteenth century, this photograph
shows the east end of Princes Street with Calton Hill in
the background. The ornamental garden in the
foreground is now the roof of Princes Mall and the
buildings directly behind were demolished to make way
for the mighty North British Hotel.*

*In the distance, perched on top of Calton Hill, the twelve
columns of what came to be known as Edinburgh's
Disgrace can be seen. This acropolis was designed by
C R Cockerell and William Playfair and was modelled on
the Parthenon in Athens. Begun in 1822 as a national
memorial to the Scots who died in the Napoleonic Wars,
the project soon ran out of money and was abandoned.*

There are several fascinating Victorian landmarks on Calton Hill and possibly the strangest of all is Nelson's Tower. Built as a memorial to the famous admiral who died at the Battle of Trafalgar in 1805, the upside-down telescope is open to the public. There are 143 steps up to the viewing platform which offers a fantastic panorama of the city and beyond.

In 1852, a large time ball was installed at the top of the tower. This was for the benefit of the seafarers at Leith. The lowering of the ball was synchronised with the firing of the One o'Clock Gun, initially by a cable and later electrically, and it helped to ensure that the port and the city kept to the same time.

Directly below the Old Town's jagged skyline sit Princes Street Gardens. Before the area was drained to make travel between the Old Town and the New Town easier, this long, narrow valley was the site of the Nor Loch. Now, with their monuments and tree-lined walks, the Gardens offer visitors and office- and shop-workers the perfect setting for alfresco lunches. And, recently, they have become one of the main focal points for Edinburgh's famous New Year celebrations.

Each year, on New Year's Eve, around 100,000 revellers, keen to experience a genuine Scottish Hogmanay, gather in the city centre for what has become the biggest street party in Europe.

The crowds can watch live bands playing on the Gardens' Ross Bandstand and, at midnight, they have a great view of the Seven Hills Fireworks, Britain's most spectacular fireworks display.

As this 1905 photo of people who have come to watch a brass band concert shows, the Gardens have long been a place of public entertainment.

One of the most famous features in Princes Street Gardens is the Floral Clock. The face and surrounding design is made up of thousands of small plants and the hands of the clock are covered in plants too. It even tells the right time. This horticultural extravaganza is used to publicise organisations and special events. In 1965, when this photograph was taken, it was the turn of the Salvation Army, which was celebrating its centenary that year.

Because of Scotland's less than clement weather, the clock is removed every winter and replanted each spring. But, in 2003, for the first time in its 100-year history, a winter clock was created to mark Edinburgh's festive celebrations.

The flag-topped clock tower of the Balmoral Hotel is one of Edinburgh's most recognisable sights. Built in 1902 by the North British Railway Company, its original name was the North British Station Hotel. The railway company's name reflected the fact that, in Victorian times, Scotland was commonly called North Britain. And, at the time, even some Scots would happily refer to themselves as North British.

In this 1952 photograph, the equally recognisable landmark behind is the Scott Monument. Bearing a startling resemblance to Thunderbird 3, this Gothic tower is the largest monument to a writer in the world. Walter Scott has belatedly been given credit for single-handedly offering the world the romantic, 'shortbread-tin' view of Scotland that made it such a popular Victorian tourist destination. It is, therefore, appropriate that the monument to the writer whose novels served to promote Scotland as a tourist destination and the hotel that benefited so much from the resulting influx of visitors should frequently be photographed together.

There has been some sort of fortification on the site of Edinburgh Castle since prehistoric times and it has been regularly extended over the years right up until the twentieth century. Now, the oldest surviving building is St Margaret's Chapel. It was built in the early-twelfth century by King David I and is dedicated to his mother.

This turn-of-the-century picture also shows the famous cannon, known as Mons Meg, which was presented to King James II of Scotland in 1457. An enormous weapon, even by today's standards, it had the potential to frighten defenders of any siege into surrender by its sheer size but it was unwieldy and difficult to transport and so was rarely used in anger.

The barrel finally burst in 1681 and, although it was repaired, the gun has never been fired since. It is now displayed on the castle's half-moon battery.

If Edinburgh's many tour guides are to be believed, one of the most frequent questions asked by visitors is 'What time does the One o'Clock Gun go off?' The firing of a cannon at precisely 1300 hours from Edinburgh Castle began as a way of giving an accurate time check to the shipping in the Firth of Forth and Leith Harbour but has now become a much-loved daily institution. If you are walking down Princes Street and notice that it is almost one o'clock, stop and look at passers-by when the 105 mm cannon goes off. Those who leap several feet in the air are the ones who don't hail from Edinburgh.

The castle's esplanade is transformed during the Edinburgh Festival into the site of the famous Military Tattoo. Appropriately enough, the length of the esplanade is said to be the maximum distance over which an arrow could be fired with an effective outcome. Being able to judge this distance accurately would have been an aid to conserving ammunition in a siege.

Edinburgh's major financial institutions have recently undertaken a startling migration. For two hundred years, George Street in the New Town was the city's economic hub. In the 1990s, however, a custom-made financial district, known as The Exchange, sprang up next to Lothian Road – a street that is home to some of Edinburgh's most rowdy watering holes.

The area is now dominated by stylish, almost futuristic, architecture. Along from the enormous Clydesdale Bank Plaza are the predominately glass offices of the banking and insurance giant Scottish Widows. And, further west, there is this piece of stunningly modern architecture – the Edinburgh International Conference Centre. Since opening in 1995, the EICC has won numerous awards and has established itself as a venue of international acclaim.

Ironically, many of the premises in George Street, left empty by the relocation, have been turned into super-pubs and George Street now gives Lothian Road a run for its money as Edinburgh's busiest party street.

This is Tanners Close in the West Port and the unassuming door with the light above it belonged to William Hare – one of Scotland's most prolific mass murderers. In the early-nineteenth century, William Hare and his partner, William Burke, lured unsuspecting victims to this address and killed them. They then sold the bodies to the infamous Dr Knox for anatomy students to learn from.

By the time the pair were caught, they had disposed of sixteen bodies in seven months. Hare sold out his partner and, in 1829, Burke was hanged. Ironically, his body was then dissected. A pocketbook made out of his skin is still on display in the police museum on the Royal Mile.

Sadly, Tanners Close, home of these grisly entrepreneurs, was demolished in 1902, not long after this photograph was taken.

Despite its incredible backdrop, the Grassmarket, in the foreground, was once one of the most downright nasty areas of Edinburgh. By the time of this 1965 photograph, the dingy tenements were long gone and today the Grassmarket is becoming an upmarket part of town, complete with designer shops and pavement cafés.

Yet plenty of reminders of the area's chequered history are still to be found. A stone circle on the pavement marks the spot where hundreds of Presbyterian rebels, known as Covenanters, were executed by Charles II. The pub behind – the cleverly named Last Drop – celebrates the fact that this was a site for public hangings. The 400-year-old Beehive Inn, arguably Edinburgh's oldest pub, still exists and so does the White Hart Inn (seen here at the left-hand end of the row of buildings). It was reputedly the favourite hunting ground of the murderers Burke and Hare.

This is Cowgatehead, the place where the Grassmarket and the Cowgate meet. The entire vicinity was notorious for its poor housing and overcrowding but the slow-shutter technique of this 1850s' photograph imparts an almost pastoral air to the area – so perhaps it's not entirely true to say that the camera never lies.

During the nineteenth century, the buildings were mainly lodging houses for the poor and, thirty years after this picture was taken, records show that one of the flats was home to the lodging-house keeper, his family, eleven Bavarian musicians, eight Italian musicians and two shopkeepers!

In 2002, a fire broke out above one of the Cowgate's many nightclubs and one of the Fringe Festival's favourite venues, The Gilded Balloon, was devastated. Edinburgh University also lost precious Artificial Intelligence research in the inferno.

Archaeologists have been sifting through the site of the fire and have found that, during the sixteenth and seventeenth centuries, addresses around the Cowgate were actually quite prestigious and their residents were mostly noble families.

This picture shows excavations being made in preparation for building the National Library of Scotland in 1938. More than anything, this picture reveals the scale of the giant bridges that circle central Edinburgh and the ingenious way in which they were hidden. The sheer brickwork face, plummeting down from the buildings in Chambers Street to the Cowgate below, is the exposed side of George IV Bridge. Normally hidden by buildings, these openings lead to myriad vaults and chambers inside the bridge itself.

The same basic scenario is repeated under North Bridge and South Bridge. This is one of the few photographs that make clear the perplexing topography of Edinburgh's 'Underground City'. The hidden vaults are certainly below one street. On the other hand, they are just as clearly above another.

No place in the city has such a potent combination of history and beauty as the sixteenth-century walled cemetery of Greyfriars Kirkyard. These hazy tombstones perfectly demonstrate the graveyard's diverse history. In the foreground is the tomb of Alexander Henderson – one of the leading Covenanters – erected in 1646. You can still see musket holes pitting the surface where soldiers used it as target practice. Behind is the mausoleum of the famous architect James Adams.

Beyond that are the gates of the Covenanters' Prison, one of the world's earliest concentration camps, where 1,200 religious rebels were held during the winter of 1672. The prison is now infamous for a different reason. The locked gate and high walls are said to contain the Mackenzie Poltergeist – who attacks unsuspecting tour parties and has become one of the best documented supernatural cases of all time.

Across the street from the pub that took his name is the statue of Greyfriars Bobby. Bobby was a Skye terrier owned by Auld Jock, long thought to be a shepherd, who died and was subsequently buried in Greyfriars Kirkyard. For fourteen years, the dog kept a vigil over his master's grave until his own death in 1872. He is now one of the world's most famous canines thanks to Eleanor Atkinson's eponymous best-seller and Walt Disney's film. Recent research has discovered, however, that the legendary story isn't entirely accurate – the dog's master, it seems, was actually a policeman.

The drinking fountain is no longer a working part of the memorial – but that hasn't dented Bobby's popularity either. Of Scotland's many heroes, Bobby's is the most photographed statue in the country.

Opened by the Queen on St Andrew's Day in 1998, the New Museum of Scotland is a stunningly beautiful building located just along Chamber Street from its older counterpart, the Royal Museum. Built in shades of pink and yellow Clashach sandstone, it sits just across the road from the famous statue of Greyfriars Bobby. In this photo, you can just see the crown of St Giles' Cathedral peeping through between the round tower and the main body of the museum.

There are six galleries telling the compelling story of Scotland and its people. Each gallery has its own special treasures from the world-famous twelfth-century Lewis chessmen to the more prosaic set of nineteenth-century golf clubs and gutta-percha golf balls. For the Twentieth-Century Gallery, it was decided that the folk of Scotland should have a say in what was included. The result is an extraordinarily eclectic mixture of items – washing machines and TVs, cars and teddies, Irn-Bru bottles and Doc Martens' boots – and each is accompanied by the contributor's reason for selecting that particular object.

Whelks – or buckies as they are known locally – are small shellfish that can be collected from the waters of the Firth of Forth. They were traditionally sold from makeshift stalls or by buckie wives – women who hauled the fishermen's catches into the city centre in creels, like the one in the foreground here, strapped to their backs.

In bygone days, these small molluscs, rather than sweets, were popular treats for Scots children. They were sold in a dish along with a pin to prise the animal out of its shell.

The buckie wives plied their trade until fairly recently. This photograph was taken in 1955 and the last buckie wife, Mrs Fairbairn, was still carrying her creel into town as late as the 1960s.

This striking 1966 photograph shows the floodlit Assembly Hall, the meeting place for the Church of Scotland's General Assembly. Recently, it also doubled as the debating chamber of the revived Scottish Parliament while the new and highly controversial parliament building has been under construction.

The hall stands at the top of The Mound – an artificial causeway that links the Old and New Towns. In the nineteenth century, a tailor, called George Boyd, built a rough wooden bridge across the Nor Loch to make access between the New Town and his Old Town shop easier. 'Boyd's Mud Brig' proved such a popular short cut that excavated materials and compacted rubbish were ordered to be dumped around it until a large and substantial bank was formed. It is estimated that two million cartloads were eventually used to fill up the dip. Then it was simply a matter of putting a road on top.

THE WINTER'S TALE & THE TROJAN WOMEN

In the eighteenth century, the city was prospering and the middle and upper classes wanted to use their wealth to move out of the crowded tenements of the Old Town.

Back in the late seventeenth century, James VII first proposed that the city should be expanded but it was not until the mid-eighteenth century, a time of comparative peace following the Jacobite Wars, that the city fathers launched a competition for plans outlining urban improvement. In 1766, the competition was won by the young architect James Craig.

One of the emphases of his design was openness and the straight streets in regular grids, linked by formal squares and crescents, could not have been in more stark contrast to the tightly packed tenements in the narrow, higgledy-piggledy streets of the Old Town where diseases were rife.

This photo shows Charlotte Square – one of the New Town's finest squares. It was designed by Robert Adam in 1791 and the statue you can see is a memorial to Prince Albert.

Now the domain of super-pubs and upmarket big-name stores, George Street – named after King George III – is a superb example of the Georgian architecture that is such a feature of the New Town. The statue to the right of centre commemorates George IV's visit to Edinburgh in 1822 – the first time a monarch had set foot in Scotland for two centuries. It would be safe to say that this one occasion, engineered by Sir Walter Scott, permanently changed the country's national identity. The Highland games were reintroduced for the visit and the wearing of tartan and kilts, banned for almost a century, became recognised as the national dress.

What makes this 1884 picture somewhat surreal is the massed ranks of the Queen's City of Edinburgh Rifle Volunteer Brigade rolling past on penny-farthing bicycles.

Sadly, this is a sight that no longer exists in Edinburgh. The lamplighter – or leerie as he used to be called – would roam the darkening streets of the capital, lighting the city's gas lamps. Introduced into a nineteenth-century city packed with dark narrow wynds and unsavoury characters, this new form of lighting was a godsend – so much so that the lamplighter, with his long pole for turning on the illumination, became something of a hero.

This aspect of the leerie was immortalised in Robert Louis Stevenson's poem 'The Lamplighter'.

For we are very lucky, with a lamp before the door,
And Leerie stops to light it as he lights so many more.

Stevenson was a sickly child and used to wait at the window with anticipation for this nightly atmospheric treat. The lamp that sparked his poetic imagination is still there, outside his childhood home at 17 Heriot Row – although nowadays it's powered by electricity.

The glass panels in the foreground of this photograph form the roof of Waverley Station. For visitors arriving in the city by train, this view is their introduction to Edinburgh. When they come up on to Waverley Bridge, they are met by a fascinating array of architectural styles from the green dome of the imposing Bank of Scotland building to the left, with the spire of The Hub, a former church that is now a popular Festival venue, just visible behind it, to the much-sought-after striking pink and white homes of Ramsay Gardens, over to Edinburgh Castle and down to the classical facade of the National Gallery of Scotland nestling in Princes Street Gardens.

Waverley Bridge is also the starting point for the many open-top tour buses that take tourists round a city teeming with landmarks.

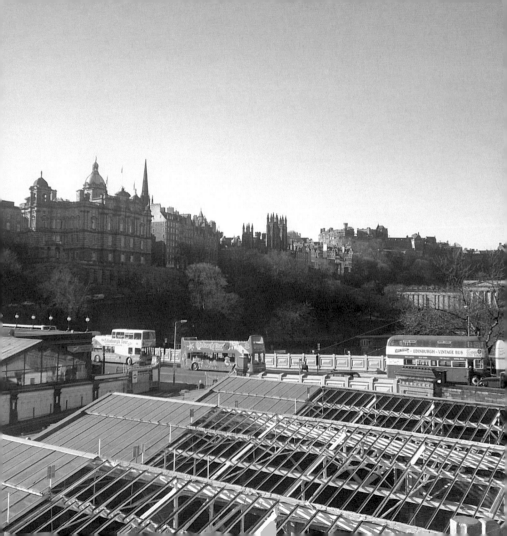

Because of massive overcrowding, Edinburgh's architects came up with some dazzling ways of packing people into small spaces. The most impressive of these were the 'lands' or 'tenements' which were, in effect, the world's first skyscrapers. In the sixteenth century, these towering buildings reached the dizzying heights of fourteen storeys – quite an achievement considering how few aids to construction there must have been at the time.

This 1857 photograph shows that the tenements still dominated the Old Town but the days of these stone giants were numbered. Four years later, a 250-year-old tenement in Bailie Fyfe's Close collapsed, burying 135 people. Famously, as rescuers pulled at the rubble, they heard a young voice crying far under the debris, 'Heave awa', lads – I'm no' dead yet!' The tragedy prompted long-overdue housing improvements and the majority of tenements in this photograph were demolished. A safer Bailie Fyfe's Close still stands, however, complete with a bust of the plucky survivor over its entrance.

Robert Cresser's Brush Shop was established in 1873 and is still going strong today. It sells every conceivable type of brush, broom, sweeper and mop and nothing else – apart from natural twine. Here, you can purchase brushes for sweeping the chimney, brushes for cleaning books and cornice and banister brushes. You can even get a churn brush, should you ever feel an overwhelming urge to clean out a milk churn. And, as the sign in the window indicates, if buying a new toilet brush is beyond your means, you can ask to have your old one rebristled or repaired!

Cresser's is situated on Victoria Street, a steeply winding road that is often overlooked by visitors. And Cresser's is not the only odd shop to be found in the area. There's a cheese shop, a shop for tall women and, possibly the strangest of all, opposite the foot of the street, there's Armstrong's – a massive second-hand emporium where you can buy everything from a World War II flying outfit to a polka-dot tutu.

Edinburgh has been blessed by a rich variety of what are politely known as 'street characters'. Of all of these, the best known is probably Coconut Tam – a street vendor during the latter part of the nineteenth century. He had a regular stance on the Royal Mile where he sold fruit, vegetables and, naturally enough, coconuts. His thin, wavery cry was instantly recognisable as he shouted his sales pitch, 'Coco-nit! Coco-nit! Come and buy – ha'penny the bit.'

His real name was Thomas Simpson and he is depicted in one contemporary account as a 'thin humpy wee man with outsize lugs supporting a frayed bowler hat which jauntily displayed a large sprig of heather'. As the photograph shows, this unflattering portrayal is actually a pretty accurate description.

This photograph, taken in Milne's Court around 1912, perfectly demonstrates the close-knit communities that existed in Edinburgh's tenements. Washing hangs from the windows and so do the occupants as they discuss the events of the day and important issues like who has and hasn't washed the stairs. Behind the group of star-struck children, who seem unsure of what do in front of the camera, is the Tolbooth Mission Hall, a reminder of the grinding poverty that once plagued the Old Town.

Milne's Court, built in 1690, was an early attempt to create a living space in the overcrowded wynds. Unusually, the design actually allowed light and fresh air to brighten these particular dwellings. This was an exception rather than a rule among the closely packed tenements that made up so much of the Old Town.

This statue of David Hume stands on the Lawnmarket, just outside the High Court of Justiciary. Erected in 1997, it was commissioned by the Saltire Society and sculpted by Alexander Stoddart. Further up the Royal Mile from the statue, just yards from Edinburgh Castle, is James Court where Hume and James Bothwell, Dr Samuel Johnson's famous biographer, both stayed.

Born in Edinburgh in 1711, David Hume is regarded by many as the greatest philosopher to have written in the English language – a thinker decades ahead of his time. His Essays Moral and Political *were part of the new economics of the time. Among other things, they advocated free trade, a subject his friend Adam Smith was also to champion. He declared himself an atheist – a dangerous ideology to hold in those unenlightened times – and his unorthodox views meant that the powers that be at Edinburgh University were never to appoint him professor of moral philosophy.*

HUME

Despite its grand name, St Giles' Cathedral isn't a cathedral at all but the High Kirk of Edinburgh. A church has stood on this spot on the High Street for over 900 years. The distinctive crown tower was erected in 1500 and, during the 1820s and 1830s, the entire building underwent a major make-over in which many of the masonry carvings and inset stone statues were added.

From St Giles's pulpit, the feared and fearsome Reformation preacher John Knox delivered his fiery sermons. Knox's house is also located on the High Street where it projects from the line of the rest of the buildings like one of the Reformation's leader's accusatory fingers.

The statue in the foreground was erected in 1685 and is the oldest equestrian statue in Britain. Astride the horse is King Charles II dressed as a Roman emperor. Odd as this choice of dress may appear, it is a definite sartorial improvement on the enormous powdered wigs, tight breeches and fancy buckled shoes that he did actually wear. The lead statue is hollow and rainwater tends to collect inside the horse until it trickles out in a rather embarrassing, if appropriate, place.

The Heart of Midlothian is a stone mosaic set into the High Street, marking the site where the old Tolbooth once stood. Built in the fourteenth century, the Tolbooth served several functions over the centuries. As its name suggests, its original purpose was for collecting tolls and, for many years, it functioned as the administrative heart of the city. As well as being one of Edinburgh's public execution sites, it was also a notorious prison. The Tolbooth was demolished in 1817 when Edinburgh's new Calton Jail opened.

It is said that, as they passed the Tolbooth, the city's criminal fraternity, a fairly large brotherhood in the days of the Old Town, would spit on its door as a mark of contempt. However, this being Edinburgh, there is also the more conservative view that the tradition of spitting on this spot was not an act of contempt for the authorities who imprisoned the wrongdoers but contempt for those inside.

Whatever its roots, it is a tradition that visitors and locals alike enthusiastically indulge in. However, many folk have no idea of the origin of this practice and some even think it is a mark of disrespect aimed at Heart of Midlothian, one of the city's two football clubs. However, the football team was not named after the High Street's heart but after a Royal Mile dance hall, called the Heart of Midlothian.

The Mercat Cross that can be seen in this 1952 photo dates from 1885 and incorporates part of the original fifteenth-century structure that stood further down the street. Traditionally, the Mercat Cross in Parliament Square is the site where important announcements are made to the public and, here, it is Queen Elizabeth II's succession that is being proclaimed.

Parliament Square, as well as being the site of the original Scottish Parliament, was a thriving place of business and also one of several execution sites in Edinburgh. It was on this spot in 1650 that Covenanter-turned-Royalist James Graham, Marquis of Montrose, met a particularly gruesome end. He was publicly hanged and then dismembered. His head was fixed on a stake at the Mercat Cross and his severed limbs were put on public display throughout the country.

Another method of dispatch used at the Mercat Cross was The Maiden – a Scottish version of the guillotine. In case it was needed in a hurry, it was kept just along the road in St Giles' Cathedral and a version of it can now be seen in the New Museum of Scotland.

There are several attractions and museums on the Royal Mile. At the very top is The Hub, a former church that is now a popular café and restaurant and, during the Festival, it acts as a ticket outlet. The Hub is an A-listed building and was formerly the Tolbooth Kirk. Just across from it is the Camera Obscura where the world outside is made to appear in a small round room. Apparently, Victorian women were frequently overcome by the experience of seeing people the size of insects moving around and a bottle of smelling salts had to be kept handy to revive them.

Further down there are museums devoted to the weaving of tartan and the making of whisky. Then there is Gladstone's Land, a seventeenth-century tenement with six storeys. It was the home of one of the Old Town's burgesses and its painted ceilings are just amazing. A brass rubbing centre sits next door to John Knox's house and across the road from it is The Museum of Childhood.

In this photo you can see the hanging sign for The People's Story Museum. It occupies the old Canongate Tolbooth and charts the lives of Edinburgh folk at work and play from the eighteenth century to the present day.

On 17 October l939, German bombers shelled the Forth Bridge and nearby Royal Navy ships. The idea of Edinburgh being attacked was so outlandish that locals dismissed anti-aircraft fire as a practice – until German bombers flew over the city. After that, defence was taken more seriously – as this 1939 picture of Blackfriars Street shows. In the end, the city got off lightly for Glasgow's heavy industry was a much more tempting target.

In a grisly way, World War II was the making of international Edinburgh. When the fighting ended, much of the continent was in ruins and the great European festivals such as Munich and Salzburg took years to re-establish themselves. Capitalising on this, the first Edinburgh International Festival took place two years after the end of the war. It was an enormous success and quickly grew to become the world's leading arts festival – a position it retains to this day.

The success of the Edinburgh International Festival led to the establishment of many other cultural spectacles, such as the Scottish Opera and the Festival Fringe. The Fringe began in 1947, the same year as the official Festival, when a few theatre companies just turned up hoping that at least some of the people who had come to see what they perceived as rather high-brow material might also be interested in watching lighter shows. That speculative few has now grown to hundreds – in fact, so successful has the Fringe become that the number of Fringe shows now easily outstrips the performances of the Festival proper.

The Fringe is rightly famous for its sheer unpredictability. Venues vary from concert halls to cars, elevators and even public toilets. Each August, the streets are swarming with street performers and people out touting for business for obscure shows. And the walking head in this picture is proof that all you need to do to put on a Fringe performance is replace the T of talking head with a W – although it probably takes a bit more creativity than this to win the annual Perrier Comedy Award.

Right at the foot of the Royal Mile is the Palace of Holyroodhouse, the Queen's official residence in Scotland, and next door to it are the ruins of the Abbey Church which was founded by David I in the twelfth century. This shot shows part of the ruins and the back of the palace. Above the roof, you can just make out the domed turrets of the palace.

Holyroodhouse was built in 1501 by James IV and, between 1528 and 1536, James V added a massive tower and a new frontage to it. For many years it was home to the troubled Mary Queen of Scots who married two of her husbands in the Abbey next door. The palace was badly damaged in a fire during the seventeenth century and, on the restoration of the monarchy, Charles II instigated a renovation programme that resulted in the basis of the building visitors can see today.

From the end of the seventeenth century until the beginning of the nineteenth, the palace was allowed to fall in to a state of disrepair. But the impending state visit of George IV forced the city to carry out some much-needed repairs. Since then, the palace has been regarded as both a home for the royal family and a place suitable for occasions of state.

This 1930 picture shows Arthur's Seat and the lower reaches of Salisbury Crags, taken from the gardens of the Palace of Holyroodhouse. They form part of Holyrood Park – 650 acres of unmanicured, mountainous land, dotted with hidden lochs. The middle of this expanse, where steep crags hide the city, is reminiscent of a scene from a Wild West movie – but the whole area is virtually in the centre of Edinburgh.

Arthur's Seat is an extinct volcano and the origins of its name are still subject to debate – though popular explanations involving the legendary King Arthur are probably misguided. It takes about two hours to get to the top but the climb is definitely worth it. The view from the summit is exhilarating – and, if the view isn't enough to take your breath away, the permanent howling wind that roars across the top certainly will be.

Taken in 1946, this picture shows a knife-grinder with his cart next to Bruntsfield Links. The operators of these carts worked the streets or went door-to-door, sharpening knives, saws, razors and scissors or repairing umbrellas and household tools. The grinding wheels can plainly be seen in the back of the cart.

Bruntsfield Links themselves are a pleasant thirty-five-acre triangle of greenery. The area can lay claim to being the site of one of the world's earliest golf courses. The game has been played here since the fifteenth century and possibly even earlier. The Links are the last remaining greenery of what was the Burgh Muir. Here, the city's cattle were grazed and, on occasion, Scottish armies were raised.

Of all the areas swallowed up by Edinburgh's eventual expansion, the burgh of Leith is the one that has held on to its own identity most fiercely. Try telling a Leither that he is actually a citizen of Edinburgh and you are by no means sure of a polite response. Once Scotland's principle port, Leith's independent status was greatly envied by the wealthy merchants of Edinburgh, who finally managed to get it incorporated as part of the city in 1920.

Situated just a couple of miles from the city centre, it was originally a fishing village but, with its rapidly growing affluent waterfront culture, its roots are becoming increasingly obscured. The converted warehouses in this photo are now expensive housing and some the city's trendiest restaurants and bars are to be found here.

The area now boasts a new shopping and leisure centre, Ocean Terminal, which is also the site of the permanent dock for the decommissioned Royal Yacht Britannia.

The Meadows has been a popular park since its founding in 1860. It separates the main buildings of Edinburgh University from the faded Victorian magnificence of Marchmont. Marchmont contains an enormous student population and, each day, an endless procession of book-carrying young academics make their way back and forth across the tree-lined walks. The Meadows has an atmosphere that is quite unique – patricularly on bleak winter days, there is a melancholy splendour that few recreational areas can match. Perhaps this is due to the fact that Edinburgh's plague victims were buried there.

This 1959 picture shows Jawbone Walk and it isn't difficult to guess where the name came from. This huge arch is comprised of whale jawbones joined together at the top and was an exhibit left over from the 1886 Edinburgh International Exhibition of Industry, Science and Art held on the Meadows. It was gifted to the city by the Zetland and Fair Isle Knitting Stand!

Corstorphine is a prosperous suburb three miles west of the centre of Edinburgh. It nestles below Corstorphine Hill, the site of the world-famous Edinburgh Zoo. Like so many of Edinburgh's locales, it too has a literary connection. The renowned Edinburgh author, Robert Louis Stevenson, chose the hill's well-known viewpoint as the place where David Balfour and Alan Breck say their farewells in the novel Kidnapped.

The Wee Shop, one of the area's landmarks, is claimed to be the smallest store in Scotland and is only four-and-a-half-feet long. Since it was built in 1902, it has been a tobacco and confectionery shop, a personal corsetry business, a watchmaker's, a shoemaker's and a coal merchant. It is currently leased to a firm of solicitors.

(THE WEE SHOP)
BRUCE LINDSAY
APPROVED COAL & SMOKELESS
FUEL MERCHANTS
PROPERTY OF THE CORSTORPHINE TRUST

Dean Village was a milling hamlet to the north of Edinburgh. For over 800 years, it depended on the strong currents of the Water of Leith to power its mills and, at one point, there were eleven of them. Today, it has undergone a remarkable renaissance. Surrounded by the city and lying 100 feet below Thomas Telford's spectacular Dean Bridge, the mill-workers' cottages and warehouses have been beautifully restored and are now much-prized residences.

Dean Village still has an isolated feel, perhaps because of the torturously steep slopes that lead down to it. The courtyard this child is gazing across has not changed since this 1954 photograph and the place retains an air of secluded antiquity. This is partly due to the clever way the newer buildings, designed in old-fashioned styles, have been integrated with the older ones.

For most of its history, Stockbridge was a small village on the banks of the Water of Leith. It enjoyed a spate of popularity in the nineteenth century when physicians of the day testified to the incredible healing powers of nearby St Bernard's Well. It has now grown into a sizeable district of Edinburgh, with a bustling and cosmopolitan character and a main street filled with a mixture of 'arty' stores, charity shops and delicatessens.

This picture of the 1900s shows a group of children in the Stockbridge 'colonies' – one of several areas of colony houses across the city. Built by cooperatives in the mid-nineteenth century, they were designed to provide inexpensive housing for working-class people. The prices of these much-sought-after homes can no longer be called cheap, by any stretch of the imagination, and the Stockbridge ones command the highest prices of all the colonies.

Known locally as just 'The Botanics', the Royal Botanic Gardens are home to around 16,000 species of plants. Highlights include a spectacular rock garden and a Chinese hillside, complete with waterfall and pagoda.

The extensive glasshouses, seen here in the background, feature five different climate zones and walking through them is a remarkable assault on the senses. The topsoil for the glasshouses came from excavations for the Forth Rail Bridge which was being built at the same time.

Towering above the rest of the glasshouses is the Tropical Palm House which, when it was built in 1834, was the highest in the country. Despite its height, the palms have to be carefully monitored in case they grow too tall and shatter the roof.

The sculpture in the foreground is the Linnaeus Monument which was designed by Robert Adam. Appropriately, it is a memorial to Carolus Linnaeus, the Swedish botanist who founded the two-term Latin naming system for classifying plants.

Fettes College, established in 1870, is a palatial building studded with pillars and gargoyles. It is often compared to the Walt Disney Magic Kingdom castle logo. The school's setting is equally impressive. Perched on a high ridge, it overlooks a truly panoramic view right across Edinburgh to the Pentland Hills.

The college has a formidable academic reputation. Prime Minister Tony Blair studied there but he is not Fettes's most famous scholar. That honour, as literary anoraks will know, goes to Ian Fleming's famous creation, Lieutenant Commander James Bond.

Just down the street is another, far less impressive, building – but with equally strong literary connections. It is Fettes Police Station, workplace of Ian Rankin's celebrated detective, Inspector Rebus.

*The imposing ruin of fourteenth-century Craigmillar
Castle guards the southern approach to Edinburgh. Its
most famous resident was Mary Queen of Scots. The
nearby hamlet, which housed her French attendants, is
still called Little France and is now the site of the new
Edinburgh Royal Infirmary.*

*The castle has quite a notorious history. It was here
that James III imprisoned his brother John, Earl of Mar,
who died in its cellars. The murder of Mary's husband,
Lord Darnley, was plotted within its battlements and
restoration work uncovered a walled-up skeleton in one
of the vaults.*

*This pastoral scene of haymaking in the 1920s is a
thing of the past and the grassy parkland has been
replaced by council housing.*

This turn-of-the century fishmarket is being held in the
fishing village of Newhaven, just to the north of the city.
Newhaven once had a very promising future. Because of
its deep harbour, it was the site chosen by James IV, in
the early sixteenth century, to launch Scotland's bid to
build a world-class navy. It was here that the largest
ship of its time in the world, the Great Michael, *was*
constructed. The forests in the Kingdom of Fife were
almost completely denuded in order to provide enough
timber for the job. Before it ever saw action the ship was
sold to the French to pay off massive debts incurred by
the Scots military disaster at Flodden.

Newhaven then went back to being the quiet fishing
village it is today and Scotland has not had much
success as a naval superpower since.

Just decades after the Forth Rail Bridge opened, the Victorian belief that trains were the transport of the future began to fade. The motoring age had dawned and ever-increasing road traffic crossing the Forth faced the choice of waiting in the queue for the ferries at Queensferry or a detour of over forty miles via Kincardine Bridge.

Even so, it was not until 1958 that work began on a road bridge. The construction was not without its hazards – seven men lost their lives before it was finally opened in 1964. This photograph shows the half-finished 'Highway in the Sky'. When it was completed, its one-and-a-half mile span made it the longest suspension bridge in Europe at that time.

Side by side, the road and rail bridges are still a magnificent sight – each representing the spectacular engineering feats of their respective centuries.

In this 1905 photograph, a steam train puffs its way across the Forth Rail Bridge. Hailed as an engineering miracle when it was opened in 1890, the bridge was designed by Sir William Arrol. As 1879 drew to a close, the rail bridge over the River Tay collapsed during a storm, taking a whole train-load of passengers to their deaths in the churning waters below, and the worry that something similar might happen to the Forth Bridge was never far away. Happily Arrol's design was sound and his success with the Forth Bridge led to him being chosen to design a new bridge over the Tay. However, the building of the rail bridge over the Forth was not completely without cost as fifty-seven men died during its construction.

96 Ferries had long been the traditional way of crossing the Firth of Forth – you can just make out the steam from a ferry's funnel in the picture. The rail bridge saw the beginning of the end of this means of transport and, when the Forth Road Bridge opened in 1964, 900 years of commercial ferry crossings ceased entirely.